Baseball
and Softball
R U L E S

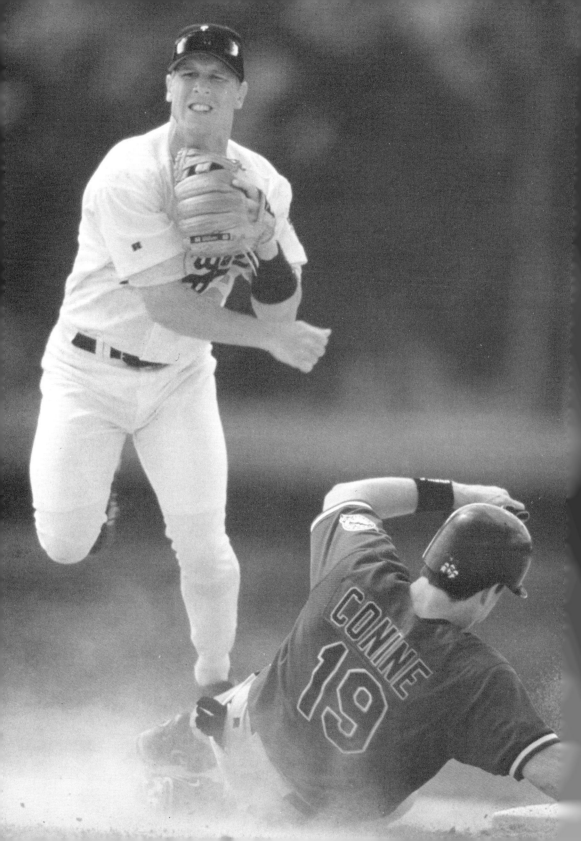

Baseball
and Softball
R U L E S

IAN SMYTH

WARD LOCK

A WARD LOCK BOOK

First published in the UK 1998
by Ward Lock
Wellington House
125 Strand
LONDON
WC2R 0BB

A Cassell Imprint

Distributed in the United States by
Sterling Publishing Co., Inc.
387 Park Avenue South, New York,
NY 10016-8810

A British Library Cataloguing in Publication
Data block for this book may be obtained from
the British Library

ISBN 0 7063 7600 5

Printed and bound in Great Britain by
The Bath Press, Bath

ACKNOWLEDGEMENTS

Cover photograph: Gary Sheffield of Marlins
playing at Wrigley Field, Chicago. © Allsport
USA/Jonathan Daniel

Photographs: Action Plus/Glyn Kirk 1;
Allsport/Simon Bruty 65, 73/Michael King 70;
Allsport USA/Al Bello 9, 28, 36/Jonathan Daniel
41, 49, 50/Otto Greule 44, 53/Jed Jacobsohn 12,
62/Doug Pensinger 56/Matthew Stockman 60.

Frontispiece: Adam Riggs (left) of the
Florida Marlins and Jeff Conine (right) of
the LA Dodgers.

CONTENTS

INTRODUCTION

Baseball and softball are currently two of the most popular team sports, perhaps because both of them are easy games to play in the local park. You need only a bat and ball and a bit of improvisation. The aim of this book is to explain the rules of both games in a style relevant to the needs of the average follower of both games. It is hoped that it will help to enhance your enjoyment of both playing and watching the sports.

Where did these two highly popular sports come from? **Baseball** is traditionally regarded as an American game, possibly derived from the game of rounders, the earliest known reference to which was made in 1744. History has it that Oliver Wendell Holmes is believed to have played a game, loosely based on the rules of rounders, at Harvard University, in 1829. He is said to have modified the playing area into a diamond shape and to have referred to the game as 'base-ball'.

Certainly it is known that 'base-ball' was played in both England and America in the early nineteenth century. The first basic rules of the modern-day game were drawn up by Alexander Joy Cartwright Junior on 23 September 1845; he also founded the Knickerbocker Base Ball Club of New York, which was the sport's first organized team.

The origins of **softball** can be traced back to 1887, when George Hancock of Chicago developed a game that could be played indoors during the harsh winter months. He also established the first code of rules but called the game 'indoor baseball'. There have been many versions of the game, but in 1932, following an American cross-regional tournament in which 30 teams played using at least 12 different sets of rules, things came to a head. As a consequence, in 1933 the Amateur Softball Association was established to govern the sport in the USA.

Around the world, new nations and fresh generations are turning to the games of baseball and softball as team games in which the individual can shine but where the full squad pulls together in the traditions of team spirit. To ensure the prosperity of both sports, their expansion must take place against a background of respect for and knowledge of their laws, and a readiness to promote and preserve sportsmanship and good etiquette.

 NOTE

For the sake of convenience and ease of reading, male terms are used throughout the book. This should be taken to imply that women do not play baseball and softball.

Both sports are now well established, and their original rules were drawn up in the age of imperial measurements. Consequently, such measures are given in imperial with the metric equivalent in brackets.

BASEBALL

A GUIDE TO THE GAME

Baseball is a bat-and-ball game played between two teams of nine players each. The object for each team is to score more runs than the opposition. A run is scored when a batter advances around all the three bases on the baseball field, finally reaching the home plate. A run can be scored in stages, so it is not essential for the batter to get all the way around on one hit. If the batter does get around on one hit, this is called a home run.

A baseball game consists of nine innings, with each team batting nine times. An inning ends when three players of the batting side are out. Each batter is allowed three strikes before being called out. Alternatively, four 'balls' (pitches that do not enter the strike zone) in a row allow the batter to 'walk' to the first base.

A strike is a pitched ball that passes over the home plate between the batter's knees and chest when a normal stance is taken up by the

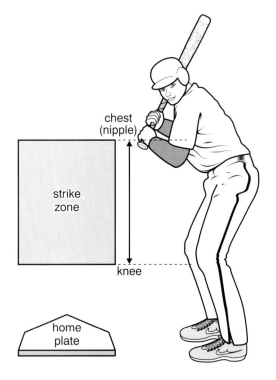

The strike zone in baseball comprises the area directly over the home plate that falls between the batter's knees and chest (the nipple).

batter. This is known as the strike zone. A strike will also be called if the batter swings and misses, whatever the location of the ball. If the batter hits the ball into foul territory, a strike will also be called, for the first two strikes only. Strikes are called by the home plate umpire, who is positioned directly behind the catcher.

A ball is called when a pitched ball is outside the strike zone, and the batter does not swing. A fair hit is a batted ball that settles in fair territory in the infield or lands in fair territory in the outfield. If a batted ball is caught on the fly by any fielder, then the batter is out.

The batter becomes a runner, provided he is not out but has finished his time at bat. A base runner is called out if the ball is held on first base before the runner reaches it. At second base, third base and home plate, the runner must be tagged with the ball, unless the runners are forced

Fielding, or defensive, positions:
(1) pitcher; (2) catcher; (3) first base;
(4) second base; (5) third base; (6) shortstop;
(7) left field; (8) centre field; (9) right field.

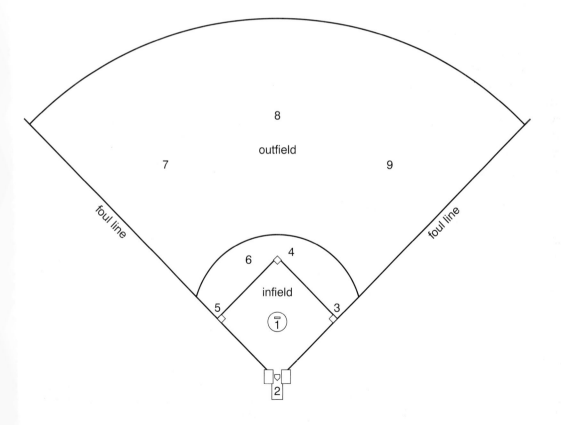

to advance. No base can be occupied by more than one runner; therefore, if there is a runner on first base and the batter hits the ball, the runner must run to second base so as to free first base for the batter. In this situation, the fielder does not have to tag the runner; he can simply step on the base with the ball in his possession.

On defence, the nine players are usually situated in the positions shown in the diagram on page 11.

The essence of the game of baseball is the duel between pitcher and batter. The pitcher has to outwit the batter using different pitches, speeds and locations. The batter's job is to get on base safely, then attempt to score. Generally, the pitcher has the upper hand with even the best batters only getting fair hits in three out of ten attempts.

A panoramic view of a baseball field.

THE FIELD OF PLAY

The baseball field is formed by two lines known as foul lines. These run from the home plate through first and third base, creating a 90-degree arc. The inner part of this segment is referred to as the infield. The outer part is called the outfield.

The infield is formed by a 90ft (27.43m) 'diamond' which has a base on each corner. Each of these bases must be touched by the runner to score a run.

The outfield is formed by the two foul lines, which should extend at least 320ft (97.5m) to reach the outfield fence. The area between the foul lines is called fair territory. The areas outside the foul lines are called foul territory.

Within the infield there are two important areas. The first is the pitcher's mound. This is a raised area from where the pitcher delivers the ball. The mound is elevated 10in (25.4cm) above the level of the home plate. It has a radius of 9ft (2.74m).

On top of the mound is a pitcher's plate (also called a pitching rubber), that measures 24in by 6in (60.96cm by 15.24in). The pitcher must be in contact with this plate when he starts his delivery.

The other important area of the infield is the home plate area. In the centre of this is the home plate, which is a five-sided piece of hard white rubber 17in (43.18cm) wide and set into the ground. Either side of the home plate is a batter's box, where the batter must stand when hitting the ball. If the batter hits the ball while being out of this box, he will be called out. Behind the home plate is a catcher's box, where the catcher fields the ball. The catcher must stay in this box until the pitcher has delivered the ball.

The field of play.

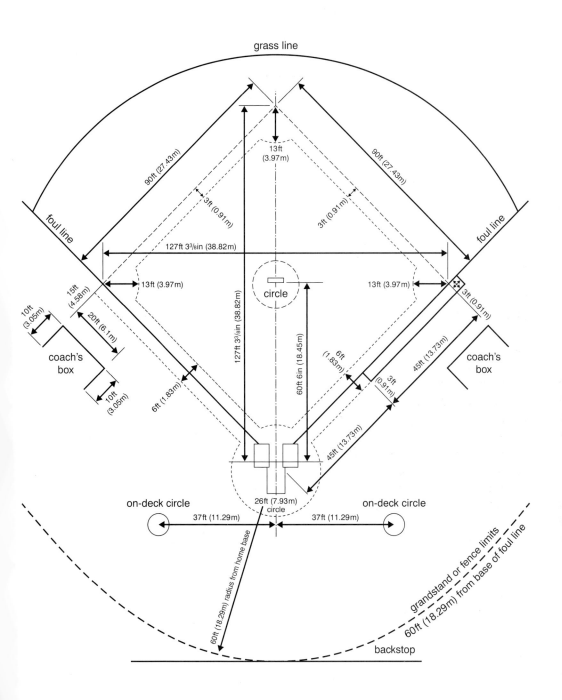

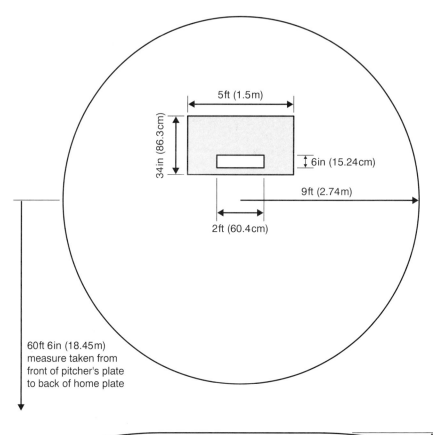

5ft (1.5m)

34in (86.3cm)

6in (15.24cm)

9ft (2.74m)

2ft (60.4cm)

60ft 6in (18.45m)
measure taken from
front of pitcher's plate
to back of home plate

10in (25.4cm)

The pitcher's mound.
Top: view from directly above – the shaded area represents the flat part of the mound.
Bottom: front view.

● FIELD EQUIPMENT

The following items of equipment are essential for playing a well-organized game of baseball.

The Home Plate

The home plate is a five-sided piece of solid rubber. It is 17in (43.18cm) wide and 17in (43.18cm) long. The home plate needs to be properly secured to the ground so that it does not move around during the course of the game.

The Pitcher's Plate

The pitcher's plate, sometimes known as the pitcher's rubber, is made out of hard white rubber. It measures 24in (60.96cm) by 6in (15.24cm).

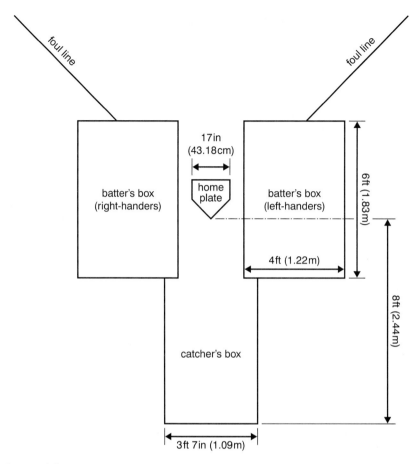

foul line

foul line

17in
(43.18cm)

batter's box
(right-handers)

home
plate

batter's box
(left-handers)

6ft (1.83m)

4ft (1.22m)

8ft (2.44m)

catcher's box

3ft 7in (1.09m)

The home plate area.

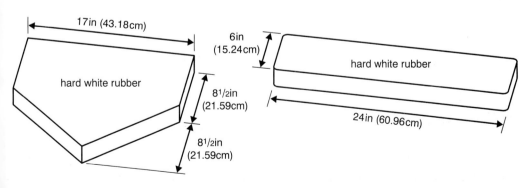

17in (43.18cm)

hard white rubber

8¹/₂in
(21.59cm)

8¹/₂in
(21.59cm)

6in
(15.24cm)

hard white rubber

24in (60.96cm)

Dimensions of the home plate.

Dimensions of the pitcher's plate or rubber.

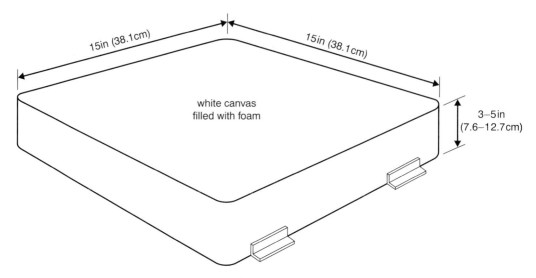

15in (38.1cm)

15in (38.1cm)

white canvas
filled with foam

3–5in
(7.6–12.7cm)

Dimensions of a base.

It is secured into the pitching mound 10in (25.4cm) above the level of the home plate. The distance from the front of the pitcher's plate to the back of the home plate is 60ft 6in (18.44m).

Bases

The three bases – first, second and third – are square pieces of white canvas 15 × 15in (38.1 × 38.1cm) and 3–5in (7.62–12.70cm) thick. They are filled with foam and secured to the ground, and are situated at the corners of the diamond.

The Backstop

Most baseball fields have some form of backstop, such as netting, to prevent the ball from flying straight past the batter into the crowd of spectators. The backstop should be at least 60ft (18m) behind the home plate. The height and width of the backstop varies, but it should be big enough to offer protection to spectators and actually stop the ball in flight.

PLAYING EQUIPMENT

As baseball is essentially a bat-and-ball game, the two main pieces of equipment are obviously the bat and ball. However, a baseball is capable of travelling at great speed and other items, including gloves, protective equipment and field equipment, are necessary for an organized, and therefore safe, game.

● BATS

The rules of baseball state that a bat is a smooth, rounded stick with a maximum diameter of 2¾in (6.9cm), and a maximum length of 42in (1.07m).

The bat handle may be covered or treated with any material or substance to improve grip. This treatment must not extend more than 18in (45.7cm) from the top of the bat. Anything longer than this contravenes the rules.

In the major leagues in America, professional baseball players are only allowed to use wooden bats, generally made of ash. Most amateurs use aluminium bats, because of their durability. They last much longer than wooden bats, and are less expensive in the long run.

Most players use bats that weigh between 28 and 34oz (0.8–1.1kg). The famous American player Babe Ruth used a bat that weighed over 3lb (1.5kg)! Beginners will probably try to use the biggest bat available, under the misapprehension that it will enable them to hit the ball harder and further. In fact, it is best for beginners to use a light bat. It will be easier to control and consequently easier to hit the ball with.

As with any sport, tampering with a bat is forbidden. Indeed, recent offenders in the professional game of baseball have been punished severely.

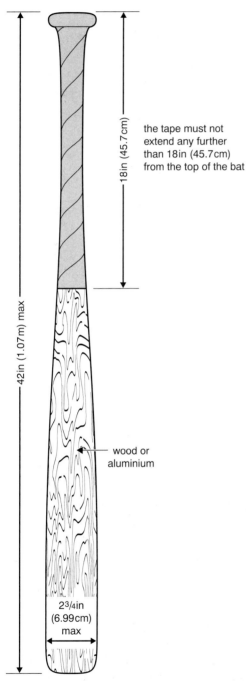

18in (45.7cm)

the tape must not
extend any further
than 18in (45.7cm)
from the top of the bat

42in (1.07m) max

wood or
aluminium

2³/₄in
(6.99cm)
max

A standard baseball bat.

● THE BALL

The ball is made from a core of cork or rubber which is first bound around with yarn and then finished off with a binding of white leather. It is round and has a circumference of 9–9¼in (22.8–23.4cm). It weighs between 5 and 5¼oz (141.7–148.8g). The ball is stitched together in such a way that two raised seams are formed. These seams are used by the pitchers to make the ball move when they pitch. Traditionally, baseballs were made in Cuba and Haiti, but most are now made in eastern Asia.

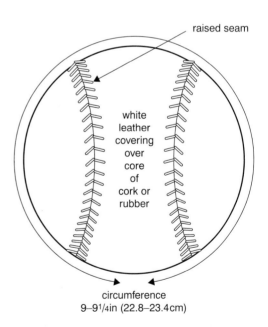

raised seam

white
leather
covering
over
core
of
cork or
rubber

circumference
9–9¹/₄in (22.8–23.4cm)

A standard baseball. The ball is made from a white leather covering over a core of cork or rubber.

● GLOVES

All fielders wear gloves while they are fielding. These gloves are made of leather, but are lightweight. They have a pocket (or webbing) which allows the fielder to catch the ball more easily. There are three main types of glove.

The catcher wears a specialized catcher's mitt, which has lots of padding to protect the catcher's hand. During the course of a game, a catcher will receive the ball over 150 times, at speeds over 90mph (145km/h). The mitt will protect the catcher's hand from damage. The catcher's mitt must not be more than 38in (96.52cm) in circumference, or more than 15in (39.37cm) from top to bottom.

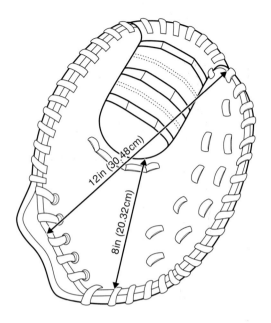

The first baseman's glove.

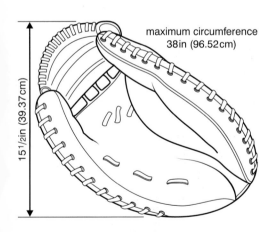

The catcher's mitt. The mitt is held out with the palm of the hand facing the batter. This way the glove may be turned over quickly and the ball retrieved by the throwing hand.

The first baseman also has a special glove, which is a little bigger than a standard fielder's glove. The mitt should be no more than 12in (30.48cm) long from top to bottom, or more than 8in (20.32cm) wide across the palm.

Infielders (including the pitcher) and outfielders wear similar gloves, although generally infielders have smaller gloves, so as to enable a quick transfer of the ball from the glove to the throwing hand. Plays in the infield have to be executed quickly; the size of the infielder's glove helps facilitate this.

The pitcher's glove cannot be the same colour as the team's uniform. It must not be white or grey, as this

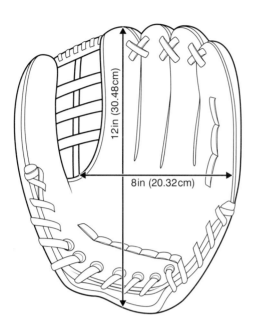

The fielder's glove.

could inhibit the batter's vision of the baseball itself. The pitcher cannot attach anything to the glove which is a different colour to the glove itself.

● BATTING HELMETS

In baseball, it is now mandatory for all batters to wear batting helmets. These are made of plastic, with foam padding, and they protect the batter from potential head injuries which could be caused by a thrown or batted ball while either batting or base running.

● CATCHER'S EQUIPMENT

Owing to the nature of his position, the catcher needs to be well protected. The catcher has to wear a helmet, a face mask, a throat protector, a chest protector, a cup (like a cricketer's 'box') and leg guards. Not without good reason are these sometimes referred to as the 'tools of ignorance'! Modern catching equipment is lightweight and user-friendly. It provides adequate protection while allowing the catcher freedom of movement.

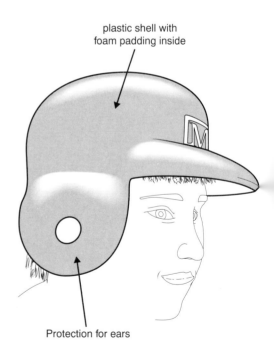

plastic shell with foam padding inside

Protection for ears

This type of batting helmet offers maximum protection.

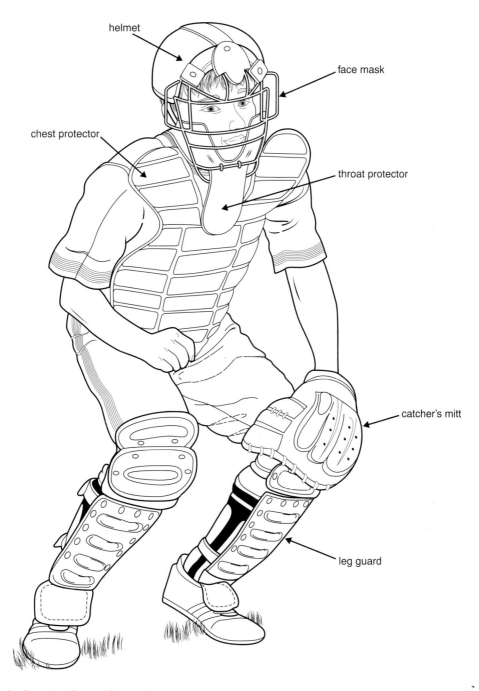

helmet

face mask

chest protector

throat protector

catcher's mitt

leg guard

The catcher's protective equipment.

● UNIFORMS

For obvious reasons, all players on a team must wear uniforms of identical colour, with numbers on the back of the shirts. No part of the uniform is allowed to bear an image or logo that resembles a baseball.

● CAPS

The wearing of caps is traditional in baseball. Indeed, in recent years baseball caps have become a fashion item. These caps usually have a logo or letter on the front of the crown. Every self-respecting ball player or fan will possess at least one baseball cap.

NOTE OF CAUTION
As a general rule, buy your playing equipment with care. Take the advice of other team members and relevant baseball magazines and purchase from reputable sports shops and companies. Buy any second-hand equipment with caution and only if you can be satisfied about its history. Remember, baseball can be a dangerous game and your personal safety is more important than a 'bargain'.

THE UMPIRES

The most difficult, yet possibly the most rewarding, role in baseball is that of the umpire. Unfortunately, umpires are often the butt of the frustration and anger of coaches, players, spectators and parents. However, without umpires the game could not be played.

Every umpire has a different motivation towards officiating. Most umpires do it as a hobby – an extension of their baseball career – once their playing days are over. It is difficult to attract umpires into the game, as indeed it is in many other sports which also struggle to find enough good people wishing to officiate.

Umpiring is a very difficult job, with the majority of decisions based on the umpire's split-second judgement. To this end, the umpire is always liable to be second-guessed by players and coaches alike. However, provided that the umpire makes his decisions firmly, fairly and consistently, games will be enjoyable for players and spectators alike.

As a sport, baseball has many little technicalities and nuances which make it both fascinating and frustrating at the same time. Unlike many other sports, baseball allows managers and coaches to appeal against the umpire's decisions on technical aspects, such as rules and rule interpretations, but not against judgement decisions. In these circumstances, umpires need to be on top of their game, having a thorough understanding and knowledge of the rules.

● EQUIPMENT

Umpires also need to protect themselves from injury, and as advised for players earlier, should purchase any equipment from a reputable supplier. Remember, only well-made and well-cared-for equipment will offer maximum protection. The plate umpire (sometimes referred to as the umpire-in-chief) is positioned directly behind the catcher, and therefore needs to wear specialized protective equipment.

Body Protectors
Most umpires today use inside protectors, worn under the shirt, rather than an outer-clothing body protector. The inside protector provides protection for the chest, shoulders and upper arms. It is important that the protector is a good fit in order to ensure the umpire's safety, and also to offer more comfort, enabling the umpire to concentrate on the task at hand. While wearing the protector, the umpire should be able to move freely and easily.

Masks
A standard umpire's mask is obviously vital for protection. Most umpire's masks are lightweight and are therefore comfortable to use throughout the whole game. Good masks provide protection to the throat area and to the side of the head. It is essential for an umpire's mask to provide excellent visibility.

Leg Guards
Leg guards provide protection for the insteps, ankles, shins and knees. The shin guard should buckle to the outside to prevent injury and enable

greater freedom of movement when running.

Shoes
The plate umpire should wear black shoes with black laces. They should have a metal toe plate to provide protection against foul balls. Base umpires should wear black trainers with black laces, or black shoes. In all circumstances, shoes should be kept in good condition and polished to promote a professional appearance.

Indicator
The indicator is a small hand-held device that the umpire uses to keep track of the count, i.e. balls and strikes, and the number of outs. It is vital that the plate umpire has an indicator. Base umpires should also have one.

Plate Brush
The plate brush is used by the plate umpire to clear the home plate of dirt and any other debris. It is vital that the pitchers, batter and umpire should be able to see the plate clearly at all times. Base umpires should also carry a brush in case a base needs clearing. The brush should be carried in the right rear pocket or in the plate umpire's ball bag (see below).

Ball Bag
The ball bag is a small bag that is attached to the plate umpire's belt. It should be large enough to hold three baseballs, and it should be black.

Pencils

A pencil is needed for marking changes to the line-up card or for noting protests or ejections.

● PREPARATIONS

It is the duty of the umpire to be well presented – in other words to look the part. A smart appearance will command respect at the ball park. The umpire's shoes should be polished and his trousers pressed, thus conveying a professional attitude and appearance. An umpire's uniform should consist of grey trousers, a pale blue shirt, an umpire's cap and black shoes.

As with the players themselves, a good umpire will be generally fit and therefore able to react to the game quickly.

In most amateur baseball games, umpires work in pairs. This two-man system involves a plate umpire and a base umpire. Their respective roles are described in detail below.

Pre-Game Duties

Before entering the field, umpires should have a thorough understanding of their own, and their colleague's, duties and responsibilities. This is crucial for coverage responsibilities, i.e. which umpire is responsible for which bases, and which of them is to make the necessary calls. It would be disastrous if both umpires called a play differently. They should be sure that they have clarified any rule interpretations between them before the game begins.

Upon arrival at the field, the umpires need to check the field of play. They should ensure that the field itself is safe to play on, conforms to league requirements, i.e. the lines are marked correctly, and that the bases, the home plate and the pitching rubber are in the correct position and are secure.

Starting a Game

Once the line-up cards (see page 32 for more details about these) have been handed to the plate umpire, the game has technically started. The umpire must ensure that all the copies of the line-up cards are identical and should receive three copies of each line-up. He should keep one for himself, give one to the opposing manager and return one to the manager.

At this point, the umpires, together with the two managers, should discuss the ground rules. These are any rules that are peculiar to that field of play. The home team manager will cover the ground rules. If the opposing manager objects to any of these rules, the umpires must make a decision.

Once the pitcher has completed his warm-up pitches, the plate umpire shouts 'Play ball' and the game proper starts.

● AFTER THE GAME

Immediately following the game, the umpires should leave the field together. They should then complete any necessary reports, and forward them to the appropriate officials.

● POSITIONING AND MECHANICS

As explained earlier, most amateur baseball games are controlled using the two-man system, with a plate umpire and a base umpire. The duties of these respective umpires are as follows.

The Plate Umpire

As the name suggests, the plate umpire is positioned behind the catcher at the home plate. His primary responsibility is to call balls and strikes.

To enable the umpire to get a good view from behind the catcher, he must assume a comfortable position. It is vital, therefore, that he assumes a correct stance. He should position himself behind the catcher, left foot

The base umpire is in position to make a call in this 1996 World Series game.

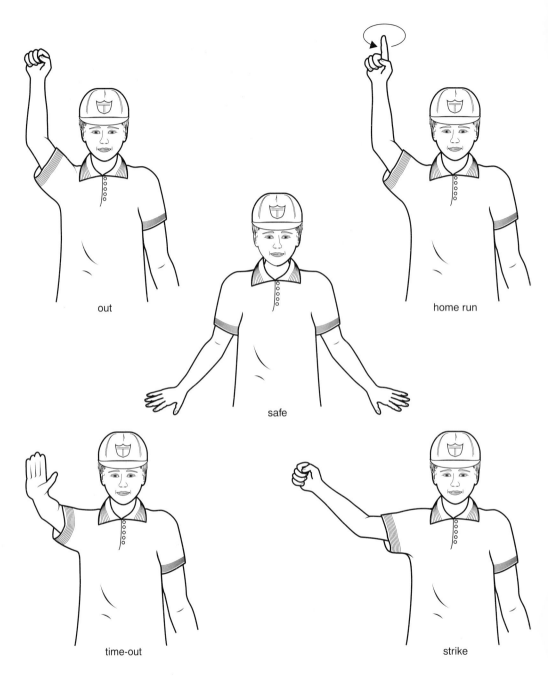

out

home run

safe

time-out

strike

Umpires' signals. These are not official, but are universally recognized.

slightly forward, with both feet facing the pitcher. This stance will ensure that all protective equipment is facing forwards – in other words, the direction where the ball comes from. It is important to bend the knees and keep the back straight. The umpire should assume a position from which he can see the entire plate. From this position, the umpire will be able to call balls and strikes.

The plate umpire may also make the call at one or more bases, as agreed before the game with the base umpire.

The Base Umpire
In the two-man system, the base umpire has a lot of ground to cover. The base umpire's job is to make the call at the bases assigned to him at the umpires' meeting prior to the game. It is vital that the umpires both know which base(s) they are responsible for, and who is to make each call.

● UMPIRE'S SIGNALS

Although the rules of baseball do not have a standardized set of umpire's signals, most umpires do use some universally recognized signals, as shown in the diagram.

● TAKING A PROFESSIONAL APPROACH

The following principles and rules-of-thumb will provide an umpire with a sound basis from which he can develop. If followed, they will serve him well throughout his umpiring career.

- Keep your uniform and equipment in good condition.
- Be courteous.
- Avoid unnecessary familiarity with players and club officials.
- Don't indulge in conversation with players on the field.
- Carry your rule book at all times.
- Keep the game moving.
- Never 'even up' mistakes.
- Keep your eye on the ball all the time it is in play.
- Wait until the play is over before making your call.
- Be in position to see every play.

SCORING

Scorers are necessary at all official baseball games. It is the scorer's job to score the game accurately, compile the official score sheet, create a box score and send the relevant statistics to the respective league officials.

Baseball is a very statistics-orientated sport, with official records for the various parts of the game stretching back over 100 years. Accurate scoring is vital in order to keep track of these records. In fact, accurate scoring goes far beyond merely keeping score of the game.

● THE SCORE SHEET

No scorer can be expected to do the job properly without a proper score sheet. Such a score sheet comprises four parts:

- the batting line-up;
- the game record;
- the box score;
- the pitching statistics.

The purpose of each of these is described in detail below.

Batting Line-up

In the section for the batting line-up, the scorer lists each player's name and his fielding position, in the order they are to bat. This batting order is given to the scorer before the game. Each team manager will hand in their line-up card. On the line-up card are listed the batters' names, shirt number and fielding positions. The scorer transfers this information onto the score sheet. There are spaces on the batting line-up for the scorer to note the introduction of any substitutes into the game.

Game Record

The game record part of the score sheet essentially records the game as

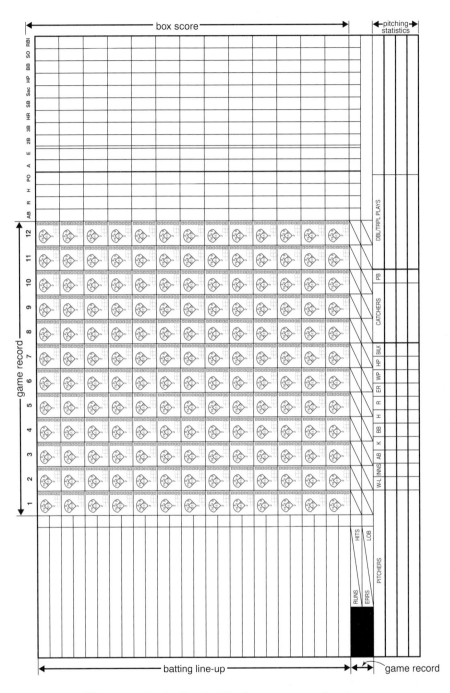

The score sheet, showing the four component parts.

it progresses. For every batter, there is a box in which the scorer marks the batter's progress around the diamond. As the batter advances from base to base, the scorer marks on the sheet how the batter or runner advanced. It is the scorer's responsibility to make judgements on hits, errors, etc. These are then recorded on the score sheet.

For each batter, the scorer records: getting on base, outs, and getting around the diamond.

The game record also has a section for recording balls and strikes. This is important and can act as a double check if there are any queries regarding the umpires' count.

Finally, in this same section, the scorer will also keep a running record for each inning of runs scored, the number of safe hits, errors by the fielding team, and the number of runners left on base.

Box Score

The box score is where the scorer lists all the relevant statistics for each team's batting and fielding performance. These box scores can be a valuable resource for coaches and fans alike, as a careful study of the score can show the nature of the game – who batted well, etc. The box score indicates the following.

- At bats – the number of times each player has an official at bat. Note that if a player is walked, sacrifices or is hit by a pitch, this does not count as an official at bat.

- Runs – the number of times a player circles the bases, returning to home plate.
- Put outs – the number of times the player actually puts out a member of the opposing team.
- Assists – the number of times a player assists in putting out a member of the opposition. (For example, if the third baseman throws a runner out at first base, the first baseman will be credited for the put out, as he actually tagged the runner or base. The third baseman will be credited for an assist, as he assisted the first baseman to make the out.)
- Errors – the number of errors each player makes. Errors are judged by the scorer. In most cases an error will be credited to a fielder if the batter should have been put out but wasn't.
- Two-base hits – every double is recorded.
- Three-base hits – every triple is recorded.
- Home runs – every home run is recorded.
- Stolen bases – the scorer determines stolen base.
- Sacrifices – a batter is credited with a sacrifice when, with fewer than two outs, he hits a fly ball and is put out, but a runner scores; or when he bunts and is put out, but a runner advances at least one base. In this instance, this does not count as an official at bat.
- Hits by a pitched ball – when the batter is automatically awarded first

base. This does not count as an official at bat.

- Base-on-balls – the number of times a batter is walked is recorded. This gain will not count as an official at bat.
- Strike outs – the number of times a batter strikes out is recorded.
- Runs batted in – a batter is credited with an RBI for every hit, sacrifice, out, error or base-on-ball which forces home a run.

The box score then gives an overall reflection of the game.

Pitching Statistics

This section of the score sheet records the details of the pitching performance, listing the following.

- The pitcher's name.
- Win or loss. To be credited with the win, a starting pitcher must complete five innings, the team must be in the lead when he is relieved and the team must not later lose the lead. For a relief pitcher to be credited with the win, he must be the most effective relief in the scorer's judge-ment, and the team must not lose the lead. The pitcher who is pitching when the team goes behind, and if that team never draws level or takes the lead, is credited with the loss. The number of innings each pitcher pitches. The number of official at bats each pitcher faces. The number of strike outs each pitcher has.

- The number of hits the pitcher gives up.
- The number of runs the pitcher allows.
- The number of earned runs the pitcher allows. Earned runs are runs that the pitcher is directly accountable for. An earned run is charged every time a runner scores a run by the aid of hits, sacrifice bunts, sacrifice flies, stolen bases, fielders' choices, walks, hit batters, balks or wild pitches. If runners score due to errors or passed balls, these are classed as unearned runs.
- The number of wild pitches the pitcher throws. A wild pitch is a pitch that the catcher cannot stop or control with normal effort, and a base runner advances.
- Hit by pitch – how many batters the pitcher hits.
- The number of balks a pitcher commits.

There is also a section in the Pitching Statistics for catchers. This notes their names and how many passed balls they allowed. A passed ball is when the catcher fails to stop a pitch that should have been stopped with normal effort, and a base runner advances. Finally, there is a section which lists double and triple plays, noting all the players involved.

When completed, the score sheet provides a very thorough compilation of statistics.

BATTING AND RUNNING

It has been said that the single most difficult skill in sport is to hit a baseball. The combination of a round bat, round ball and pitchers using different speeds, locations and trajectories on the ball make hitting a baseball very difficult. It is well worth remembering that even the best hitters in the major leagues will only hit the ball safely in three out of every ten attempts.

Each player on the offensive team must take his turn at bat in the place that his name appears on the batting line-up. The batter takes his position in the batter's box when it is his time to bat. If a batter refuses to take up his position in the batter's box, the umpire orders the pitcher to pitch, and calls strike on each such pitch. The batter can take up his position after any such pitch, and the count continues.

New York Yankees' player, Wade Boggs, ready at the plate.

● TIME AT BAT

The batter has legally completed his time at bat when he is put out, or becomes a runner.

The batter is out in any of the following circumstances.

- His fair or fly ball is legally caught by a fielder.
- A third strike is legally caught by the catcher.
- A third strike is not caught by the catcher when first base is occupied with fewer than two outs. This rule is intended to prevent a double play. For example, a catcher may deliberately drop the ball so that the runner is obliged to run. If first base is occupied, that runner is obliged to run. The catcher can then initiate a double play by throwing the ball to second base, who could then tag the base and relay the ball to first base. So, to stop this

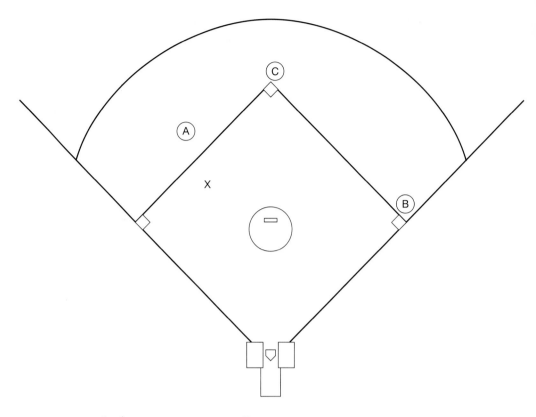

occurring, the batter is automatically out.

- He bunts foul on third strike.
- An infield fly is called. This is when there are runners on first and second base, or the bases are loaded with fewer than two outs. If the batter hits a routine fly ball to the infield, the batter is automatically called out. This rule is intended to prevent the defence from deliberately allowing the ball to drop, and thereby making a double or even triple play.
- He attempts to hit a third strike and the ball touches him. If the ball touches the batter and he does not

The infield fly rule. The batter hits the ball to position X. The plate umpires call it an infield fly because it can be easily caught, probably by shortstop A, and the batting side has runners B and C on the first two bases. As we saw earlier, a) a batter is out if caught, and b) a runner cannot run until the ball is caught. In the case of the infield fly, if caught the batter is out, and runners B and C can stay safely on their bases. If shortstop A deliberately or otherwise drops the catch, the batter would have to run to first base, which would then force B and C off base. By virtue of his position on the field, shortstop A could possibly put out two, or even three, men, and thus gain an unfair advantage by not making the catch. The infield fly rule, therefore, states that the batter is out whether the ball is caught or not. Runners B and C don't then have to leave their bases.

swing, he is entitled to walk to first base. However, if he swings and the ball hits him, it is a strike. If this happens on a third strike, the batter is out.

- His fair ball touches him before it touches a fielder. If the batter hits a ball fair and he touches the ball on his way to first base, either intentionally or unintentionally, he is out. This rule prevents the batter interfering with the path of the ball and the fielding team attempting to make a play.
- After hitting or bunting a fair ball, his bat touches the ball a second time in fair territory. This is very similar to the case above.
- After hitting or bunting a foul ball, he intentionally deflects the course of the ball in any manner while running to first base.
- After a third strike or after he has hit a fair ball, he or first base is tagged before he touches first base. When the batter hits the ball in fair territory, he is obliged to run to first base. He is only safe when he reaches the base. If the base is tagged before he arrives, he is forced out. If he is tagged, the batter is tagged out.
- In running the last half of the distance to first base, he runs out of the alley, and in the umpire's opinion interferes with the fielder attempting to make a play. The alley is a running track that is marked 45ft (13.5m) up the base line. It is essentially there for safety reasons.

If the runner runs in the alley he will touch the outside part of the first base, leaving the inside part of the base for the first baseman. This usually prevents collisions. If the runner does not run in the alley, and is deemed to have interfered with the fielder, the umpire calls him out.

- He hits a ball while one or both of his feet are outside the batter's box. The batter is obliged to hit from inside the batter's box. Often, with a junk ball pitcher (i.e. one who throws a lot of off-speed pitches), a batter may try to stand as far forward in the box as possible to try to hit the ball before it breaks. If he hits the ball while out of the box, the umpire calls him out.
- He steps from one batter's box to the other while the pitcher is ready to pitch.
- He interferes with the catcher's fielding or throwing while stepping out of the batter's box. This is to prevent the batter from helping any base runner. If the batter is deemed to have interfered with the catcher, the base runner is sent back, and the batter is given out.
- He uses or attempts to use a bat that, in the umpire's judgement, has been altered or tampered with in such a way to improve the distance factor, or cause an unusual reaction of the baseball. In professional baseball it has been known for players to put cork in their bats, by drilling out the bats

and replacing the wood with cork. This makes the bat lighter and easier to swing quickly. Quite simply, if a player is caught with an illegal bat, he will be ejected from the game. As explained earlier, at the amateur level, most baseball players use aluminium bats and consequently this problem rarely occurs.

- On appeal, if he has batted out of turn; in other words, if a batter bats out of turn in the batting order.

● RUNNERS

The batter becomes a runner and is entitled to first base in the following circumstances.

- When four balls have been called by the umpire. This is known as a walk or a base-on-balls.
- When the batter is touched by a pitched ball. This is intended to dissuade pitchers from throwing directly at batters, and the penalty is that the batter gets first base. The batter has to make an attempt to get out of the way of the ball.
- When any fielder interferes with the batter. This is usually catcher's interference, such as when the catcher's glove makes contact with the bat during the batter's swing. In this instance, the batter is entitled to first base.

The batter becomes a runner when:

- he hits a fair ball;
- the third strike is not caught, providing first base is not occupied, or there are two outs;
- he hits a home run;
- a fair ball is deflected by a fielder into foul territory.

If the batter puts the ball into play, he must run to first base. He cannot elect to receive another pitch. If the batter hits the ball safely, i.e. it is not caught, and reaches first base, this is known as a single. If he reaches second base, this is known as a double. If he reaches third base, it is called a triple. If the batter advances all the way around the bases with one hit, it is called a home run.

As the batter advances around the bases, he must touch every base in turn. Should the batter or runner fail to touch the bases, the fielding team can appeal. If the umpire also deems that the runner failed to touch a base, the runner is given out.

When running the bases, the runner must not run more than 3ft (90cm) away from a direct line between the bases to avoid being tagged. A runner is called out if he intentionally interferes with a thrown ball, or hinders a fielder making a play on a batted ball. He is also called out if he is hit by a batted ball in fair territory.

Safe or out? The base runner heading for first base.

The runner is out if he is tagged when the ball is live, while off the base. He is also out if he fails to reach the next base before a fielder tags either him or the base. A base runner cannot pass any preceding runner – if he does, he is out.

If the ball is hit into the air and is caught, the base runners must return to the base they were occupying before they can advance. For example, if there is a base runner on third base, and the batter hits a long fly ball to the outfield, the base runner will 'tag up'. This means he will stand on third base until the ball is caught. If he feels the ball has been hit far enough, he may attempt to run home, once the ball is caught. If the runner leaves third base, and the ball is caught, he must return to third base. In this situation, if the defence throw the ball to the base before the runner returns, the runner is called out.

If the runners feel that a long fly ball will not be caught, they can gamble and leave the base. However, if a fielder does make the catch, they have to return to the base.

If the batter hits a fly ball to the infield with runners on first and second bases, or bases loaded, with fewer than two outs, the umpire will call an 'infield fly'. In this instance, the batter is automatically out if the ball is fair. The defence do not even have to catch the ball. This is done to prevent the defence from deliberately allowing the ball to hit the ground, and attempt a triple play.

PITCHING

The pitcher is the player who has responsibility for pitching the ball to the batter. A good pitcher will have a major influence on any game. It has been said that a good pitcher will always outplay a good batter, but a good batter will destroy a poor pitcher.

There are two legal pitching positions: the wind-up and the set position. Either position can be used at any time.

can take one step backwards and one step forwards with his non-pivot foot in making his delivery.

From the wind-up position, the pitcher may: deliver the ball to the batter; step and throw to a base in an attempt to pick off a runner; or disengage the rubber. In disengaging the rubber, the pitcher must step off with his pivot foot.

THE WIND-UP POSITION

In the wind-up position, the pitcher must stand facing the batter, with his pivot foot on the pitcher's plate (or rubber). From this position, any natural movement associated with his delivery of the ball to the batter commits him to the pitch. The pitcher

SET POSITION

The set position is indicated by the pitcher when he stands facing the batter with his entire pivot foot on, or in front of, and in contact with the pitcher's plate, holding the ball in both hands in front of his body, and coming to a complete stop. From the set position, the pitcher may: deliver the ball to the batter; throw to a base; or step backwards off the pitcher's

late with his pivot foot. After ssuming the set position, any natural notion associated with his delivery of ne ball commits him to the pitch.

When a pitcher takes his position at ne start of an inning, or relieves nother pitcher, he is allowed to throw maximum of eight warm-up pitches. hese pitches should not take more nan one minute in total.

When the bases are unoccupied, the itcher must deliver the ball to the atter within 20 seconds of receiving . Each time the pitcher delays the ame, the umpire may call a ball. The ntention of this is to speed up the ame.

THE PITCHER ND THE BALL

nder no circumstances is the pitcher lowed to alter the condition or nature the ball. The pitcher is allowed to rub ne ball with his bare hands. However, cannot do any of the following.

Bring his pitching hand in contact with his mouth or lips while in the 18ft (5.48m) circle surrounding the pitcher's plate. This is intended to prevent the pitcher from applying saliva to the ball. Such a ball would have its flight altered in the air.

nnis Martinez of the Cleveland Indians ching from the stretch.

At one time, before they were made illegal, such balls were known as 'spitballs'.

- Apply a foreign substance of any kind to the ball. As with 'spitballs', coating a ball with something like petroleum jelly can alter the nature of the ball, giving the pitcher an unfair advantage.
- Expectorate on the ball, either directly or via his hand or glove.
- Rub the ball on his glove, person or clothing. Unlike the bowler in cricket, baseball players are not allowed to try to shine the ball. In fact, the umpires rub up the balls with dirt before the game to take away any shine.
- Deface the ball in any manner. As mentioned earlier in respect of bats, if a ball is cut or sliced, the umpire will remove the ball. Obviously this is because a defaced ball will react differently in the air.

The penalty for violation of any of the above points is that the umpire calls a ball and officially warns the pitcher. If the pitcher re-offends in the same game, he is automatically ejected.

- Have on his person, or in his possession, any illegal item or substance. Major league pitchers have been known to carry sandpaper, nail files and many other devices for the purpose of altering the nature of the ball. The penalty for being caught with such an item or substance is immediate ejection from the game.

● DANGEROUS PITCHING

The pitcher is not allowed to throw the ball at the batter intentionally. This is obviously very dangerous, and can be used as a means of intimidation. If, in the umpire's opinion, such a violation occurs, he may:

- eject the pitcher from the game;
- warn the pitcher and his manager that any further violation will result in the ejection of the pitcher and manager;
- officially warn both teams.

● BALKS

A balk is an illegal action by the pitcher with a runner or runners on base. Balks are essentially aimed at preventing the pitcher from intentionally deceiving the offensive team.

Examples of balks include the following situations.

- The pitcher, while in contact with the pitcher's plate, makes any motion naturally associated with his pitch and fails to make the delivery. Therefore, if a pitcher makes to deliver the pitch, he must go through with the delivery. He cannot start the pitch and then decide to throw to a base.

- The pitcher, while in contact with the pitcher's plate, feigns a throw to first base, and fails to make the throw. If the pitcher starts to throw to first base, he must actually make the throw. If he fails to, a balk is called.

- The pitcher, while in contact with the pitcher's plate, fails to step directly towards a base before throwing to the base. If there is a runner on first base, the pitcher cannot step towards home plate and throw to first base.

- The pitcher, while in contact with the pitcher's plate, throws to an unoccupied base. If there is a runner on first base, he may be stealing on the pitcher's first move. This rule prevents the pitcher from throwing to another fielder instead of the catcher. For example, if the runner decides to steal second base, the pitcher may realize but he must go through with the pitch. (Without this rule the pitcher could throw the ball to the third baseman or shortstop, who could then relay it on to the second baseman to tag out the runner.)

- The pitcher makes an illegal pitch.

- The pitcher delivers the ball to the batter while he is not facing the batter. Again, this rule is to prevent the pitcher from pitching while the batter is not ready to receive the pitch.

- The pitcher makes any motion naturally associated with his pitch while not in contact with the pitcher's plate. This ploy would only be used deliberately to deceive any base runners, therefore it is illegal.

- The pitcher unnecessarily delays the game. This rule is to keep the game moving along at an entertaining pace for both the players and the spectators.
- The pitcher, while in contact with the pitcher's plate, accidentally or intentionally drops the ball.
- While giving an intentional walk, the pitcher delivers the ball while the catcher is not in the catcher's box.
- The pitcher, while delivering from the set position, fails to come to a stop. The pitcher must come to a stop, so that the batter and base runner both know that he is to deliver the pitch.

The penalty for any of the above balks is that the ball is dead, and all runners advance one base. If there is a runner on third base, he will advance to home plate and score a run.

FIELDING

Fielders are divided into two categories: infielders and outfielders. All fielders need to be able to catch the ball and throw it accurately. It is the role of the defensive team to field the ball. Their aim is to prevent base runners from advancing to the home plate. However, in doing this they must abide by certain rules. Baseball allows each fielder to wear a fielder's glove. This makes fielding a little easier than if the players were using bare hands, as they did in the early days of the sport.

If a fielder deliberately touches a fair ball with his cap, mask or any part of his uniform detached from its correct place, the batter is entitled to third base. If there are any runners on the bases after such a manoeuvre they automatically score. However, in this instance the ball is still live, and the batter/runner may try to advance to the home plate at his own risk.

If the fielder throws his glove and it touches a fair ball, the batter is also entitled to proceed to third base and, as in the previously given scenario, the ball is live. In this instance, the umpire must rule that the glove actually touched the ball. If the glove does not touch the ball, no offence has occurred and the ball is live.

There are rules that also pertain to thrown balls. Should a fielder deliberately touch a thrown ball with his cap, mask or any other part of his uniform that is detached from its correct place, the batter is then entitled to two bases. As with the previous situations, the ball is live. Similarly, if the fielder throws his glove and it touches a thrown ball, the batter is entitled to two bases, and again the ball is live.

If a fielder throws the ball out of play, the batter is entitled to two bases. Therefore, if the batter hits a ground ball to the shortstop who,

An infielder fielding a ground ball.

A spectacular catch in the outfield by Reggie Sanders of the Cincinnati Reds.

trying to throw the runner out at first base, subsequently throws it over the first baseman into the crowd, the batter/runner is entitled to second base. All runners are entitled to two bases. If the wild throw is the first throw made by an infielder, the awarding of the bases shall be determined by where the runners were at the time of the pitch. Therefore, if a runner was on first base, he will be awarded third base. If there was a runner on second base, he shall be entitled to go home, and score a run. However, if the wild throw is made by an outfielder, the awarding of bases shall be determined by the position of the base runners. The timing of the wild throw is judged from when the ball leaves the thrower's hand.

OBSTRUCTION

In baseball there are various rules governing obstruction. These are in place to protect both fielders and base runners, and to allow them either to field the ball or to advance to a base fairly. A base runner is out in the following situations.

- When he runs more than 3ft (90cm) from a direct line between the two bases in an attempt to avoid being tagged, unless his action is to avoid interference with a fielder fielding a batted ball. This rule prevents a base runner from trying to run around a fielder who is attempting to make a tag.
- When he intentionally interferes with a thrown ball. If the runner does this, he is called out. If there are fewer than two outs, the batter/runner going to first base is also called out.
- When he hinders a fielder attempting to make a play on a batted ball. In this instance, the runners will be out whether the interference was intentional or not.
- Where there are fewer than two outs and a runner on third base. The runner is out if the batter hinders the fielder making a play at home plate. This rule prevents a batter blocking a catcher from tagging out a runner who is trying to score.
- When any batter or runner who has just been put out hinders or impedes any following play being made on the runner. In such circumstances, the runner is given out.
- The players' coaches or any member of the offensive team must vacate any space needed by a fielder who is attempting to field a batted or thrown ball. If they do not, interference is called and the batter/runner on whom the play is being made is called out.

Jim Thome of the Cleveland Indians slides into second base.

SUSPENDED GAMES AND FORFEITS

● SUSPENSION

A game can be suspended for many different reasons, including the following.

- Darkness. For obvious reasons, when the sport depends on such a hard ball, it can be dangerous to continue to play if the light is bad. In professional baseball, floodlights are used. However, at the amateur level most clubs do not have such expensive lighting.
- Bad weather – including heavy rain. The game may be suspended if it is impossible or dangerous to continue.

A suspended game should be resumed at the exact point of play at which the original game was halted. The line-up and batting order of the teams should be exactly the same as before the suspension.

● FORFEITS

A game may be forfeited to the opposing team when a team:

- fails to appear on the field, or refuses to play within five minutes after the umpire has called play;
- uses tactics intended to delay or shorten the game;
- refuses to continue play during the game;
- after an umpire's warning, persistently violates the rules of the game;
- fails to remove a player ejected from the game;
- refuses, or is unable, to field nine players on the field of play.

RULES CLINIC

To reinforce the information given in this book, and to clarify some of the nuances of baseball rules, this Rules Clinic answers questions commonly asked by amateur players.

I understand about 'balls' and 'strikes', but what would happen if a pitch hit the ground and then passed through the strike zone; would that be a ball or a strike?
It would be a ball. If such a delivery hit the batter, then he would be entitled to an automatic walk to first base.

Can a catch be made with the player over a boundary line or fence?
Yes. Unlike with cricket, the catch would be good. If, however, a player makes a catch and then drops the ball as a result of running into a boundary fence it is not a catch.

Does the same player start each new inning at bat for his team?
No. The batting order is in strict rotation. If the player number 7 was the last man at bat in the previous inning then number 8 starts the batting when his team next goes to bat.

If a batter is on two strikes and he hits into foul territory, is he out?
No. Normally, balls hit into foul territory are called strikes, but if a batter has two strikes against him a ball into foul territory will not be called a third strike. However, if the batter plays a bunt which goes into foul territory, it is called a strike.

Does the batter have to stand with both feet in the batter's box, or does he just need to have one foot in?
He must have both feet in the box. If he hits a ball while one or both feet are outside the box, he is given out.

I have sometimes seen a batter have three strikes against him but still become a runner. How can this happen?

If the catcher fails to catch the ball after a third strike, the batter is not out and becomes a runner, but only if *either* the first base is unoccupied *or* the first base is occupied with two men out.

Can a batter or runner deliberately cause interference with a fielder in order to help advance his own players?

No. Also, if a player is ruled out for interference, all runners must return to the last base they legally touched before the interference.

Is a ball that has been hit into the crowd used again?

Not in Major League baseball, but in the amateur game it is a different story. Balls are quite often used until they are virtually unplayable.

Are all balls that are hit out of the playing field home runs?

No. If the ball passes over the boundary fence at a distance of at least 250ft (76m) from the home base, then it is a home run and the batter is entitled to complete a circuit of the bases without risk of being put out. But, if he hits a fair fly ball out of the field at a point less than 250ft (76m) from home base, then he is only entitled to walk to second base. Before each game, the manager or coach of the home team advises the umpire-in-chief and the opposing manager or coach of special ground rules relating to the playing field.

Please clarify the infield fly rule. Why is it that a player cannot deliberately make the catch?

First, a batter who hits a ball that the umpire calls an infield fly is automatically out if the ball is fair. The rule only applies when first and second bases or first, second and third bases are occupied with fewer than two outs, and in the opinion of the plate umpire the ball could be caught by an infielder without difficulty. If the rule did not apply, the fielder could deliberately drop the ball, which would mean all runners would be forced to move off base because the batter would have to go for first. Deliberately dropping the ball therefore would give the fielder the advantage of a possible double, or even triple, play. Consequently, when an infield fly is called, the ball is deemed to be caught, and runners take the same risk as with a normal catch.

Does the batter have to hit a pitch?

No, but once he does, and the ball goes into fair territory, he must drop his bat and run.

Previous pages: A lucky Texas Rangers' fan will get to keep a home-run ball in this Major League game.

When is the ball dead?

When the plate umpire calls 'time', which may be for a variety of reasons. The ball may be damaged, he may have seen an infringement, weather conditions may make it necessary, or a manager/coach may have called for 'time-out'. Once the ball is dead, the batting side may not run, score runs, or be put out. The ball is also dead when it hits a batter or runner, or is touched by a spectator while in play.

If a fly ball lands in fair territory and then bounces into foul territory is it a fair or a foul ball?

If it lands on the infield between home and first base, or home and third base, and then goes into foul territory before first or third base without hitting a fielder or umpire, then it is a foul ball. If it first lands on or beyond first or third base in fair territory, and then goes into foul territory, it is a fair hit.

What happens if a pitch hits the batter?

It hurts! The batter is also entitled to walk (or hobble, depending where the ball hit him!) to first base and all runners, if forced, advance one base. The exceptions are when a batter is hit in the strike zone, in which case a strike is called, or when the batter does not make a reasonable effort to avoid the pitch.

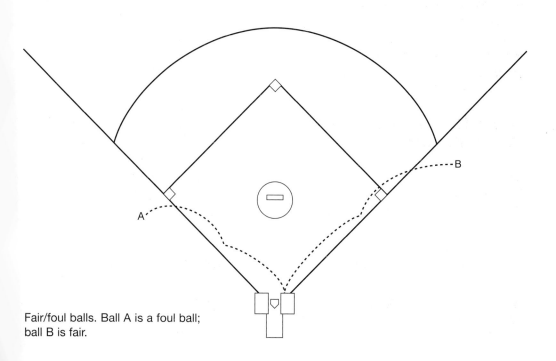

Fair/foul balls. Ball A is a foul ball; ball B is fair.

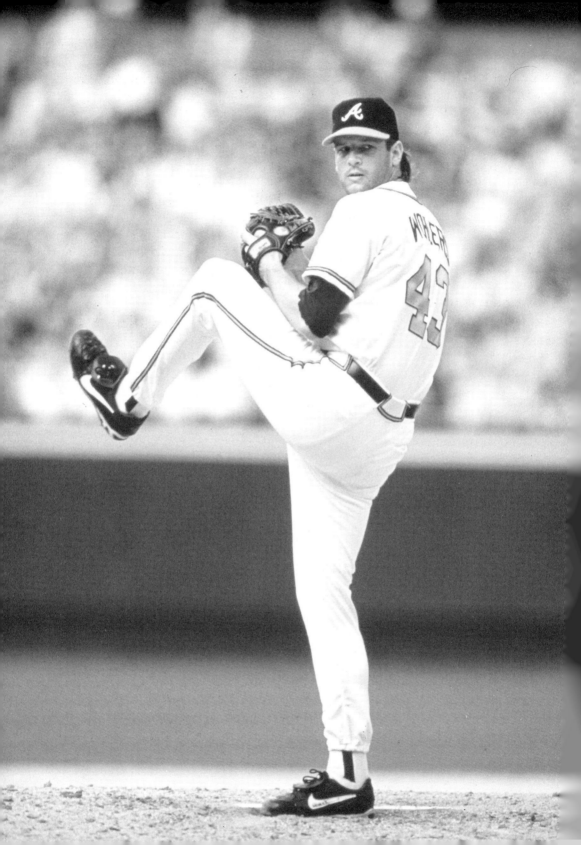

A pitcher must stand facing the base he is throwing to. But what if he doesn't?
He will be penalized by the umpire calling a balk. In every case the pitcher must step directly towards the base to which he is throwing.

Can a substituted player return to the game at a later stage?
No. Once he is taken out of the game that is it, he stays out.

Is a runner allowed to vary more than 3ft (90cm) from the direct line between bases?
No. He cannot wander all over the field of play in order to avoid a tag. However, the only exception is when he has to avoid a fielder attempting to recover the ball. In this case he may run round him and outside the 3ft (90cm) line.

What happens if a base is accidentally moved from its original position?
The runner should aim towards the original position of the base, rather than its new position, if it is unreasonably out of position. A runner is not out if a baseman tags the base at its new position.

What is the ruling if a balk is called?
If there are runners on base, each advances one base.

The pitcher in the set position, facing the batter.

If I drop my bat and the ball rolls against it, is it a penalty?
If, in the opinion of the umpire, it was unintentional and it did not interfere with the course of the ball, then the ball is live and in fair play.

A player cannot use his cap, or other pieces of clothing or equipment, to field a ball, but is it still a penalty if a fielder throws his cap at a ball and misses?
Perhaps surprisingly, no.

Can a runner intentionally kick or interfere with a batter or thrown ball so as to hinder the fielder?
No. If he does, he is out.

Can a runner overtake another runner?
Only if the runner in front is out; otherwise, you cannot go past another runner.

Common sense says that the pitcher should not pitch directly at the batter, but what if he does?
The umpire warns the pitcher and his team manager that any future violation will result in his being removed from the field. If a pitched ball hits the batter, he is entitled to walk to first base. If he is hit while making no attempt at the ball and makes no effort to get out of the way, then it is only a ball. However, if the batter is hit in the strike zone, then that is his fault for being there, and a strike is called.

What happens to runners who have left their base when a fly ball is caught?
They have to return to their original base, at risk of being tagged. They cannot run until the ball has been caught. Rarely will you see leading professionals leave their base when a fly ball has been hit because there is little risk of it being dropped.

Why don't you see pitchers shine the ball by rubbing it on their trousers like bowlers in cricket?
Because they are not allowed to. They are not allowed to deface the ball in any way, and that includes rubbing it on their clothing. They should not do anything to it that is likely to affect its true flight..For any violation, the umpire calls a 'ball', and for subsequent offences the pitcher is likely to be removed from the game.

If a runner is attempting to 'steal' but decides against it, does he or the base have to be tagged in order for him to be put out?
The runner.

If one or more runners advance bases after a hit which subsequently goes foul, can they hold their base or do they have to return?
The ball is dead and consequently they cannot run. They have to return, but cannot be put out.

Here, the runner going back to first base. The fielder would have to tag him to get him out.

Is a relief pitcher allowed some warm-up throws?

Yes, even though he will have been pitching regularly in the 'bullpen' before coming on. Once he arrives at the mound, he is allowed a maximum of eight practice pitches to his catcher.

If a side has two men out and the runner on third reaches home but the batter is put out before he reaches first base, would the run score?

No. Likewise, if a runner reached home and a runner behind him incorrectly touched a base, he would be out and the run would not count.

If a runner is off his base and a batted ball hits the base, is the runner out?

No. He can only be put out if the base is tagged by a fielder.

Why does the pitcher sometimes deliberately pitch four balls without making any effort to obtain strikes or allowing the batter the chance of a hit?

It is a tactical play. The team manager, on seeing which of the opposing team is next to bat, instructs his pitcher to take this action. The manager may feel it better to let the batter walk to first base than risk his making a successful hit.

SOFTBALL

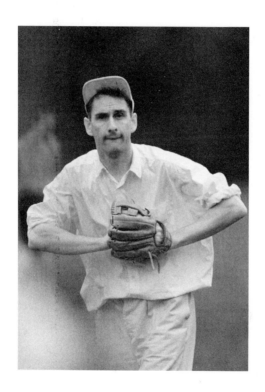

A GUIDE TO THE GAME

The sport of softball (which was originally played indoors) is essentially a derivative of baseball, and its origins can be traced back to 1887. There are now two types of softball: fast-pitch and slow-pitch. The names are derived from the different ways in which the ball is pitched.

● PLAYING EQUIPMENT

Bats
Softball bats are smaller than baseball bats, with the maximum length being 34in (86.36cm), the maximum diameter being 2¼in (5.72cm), and the maximum weight being 38oz (1.07kg). The safety grip should not extend further than 15in (38.1cm) down the handle.

A player in the women's slow-pitch team. In this recreational game the players wear uniform shirts and shorts.

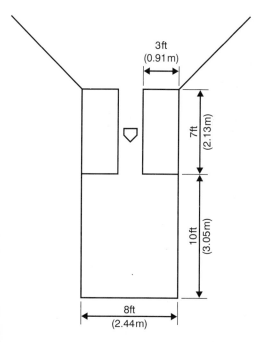

Dimensions of the home plate area for fast-pitch softball.

Ball
The ball has a circumference of 11⅞–12⅛in (30.16–30.8cm). It weighs between 6¼ and 7oz (177.2–198.5g). Hence it is bigger and heavier than a baseball.

Gloves
As in baseball, all players wear gloves. On average, the gloves are slightly larger than baseball gloves, so as to accommodate the larger ball.

Protective Equipment
In fast-pitch softball the catcher wears the same protective equipment as in baseball (see pages 22–23). Similarly, helmets should be worn when batting in fast-pitch.

● DEFENSIVE POSITIONS

The defensive positions are essentially the same as in baseball (see pages 11–12).

● HOME PLATE AREA

The pitcher's plate, home plate and bases are the same as in baseball (see pages 16–18). However, the home plate area is slightly different. The batter's box, at 3ft by 7ft (0.91m by 2.13m) is longer and thinner when compared to that in baseball. The catcher's box, at 8ft by 10ft (2.44m by 3.05m) is much larger than its baseball counterpart.

FAST-PITCH SOFTBALL

Fast-pitch is an underarm version of baseball. All the other aspects of the game, including the techniques, are the same as those in baseball. Fast-pitch games are usually played in single-sex teams, each of nine players. A coin toss decides which team bats first, and each game consists of seven innings. The scoring system is exactly the same as that of baseball, with the team scoring the most runs being the winners. The major difference is that in fast-pitch softball runners can only steal bases when the ball leaves the pitcher's hand in the delivery.

● STRIKE ZONE

The strike zone is slightly larger than that in baseball. It extends from the batter's knees to the armpits in the normal batting stance.

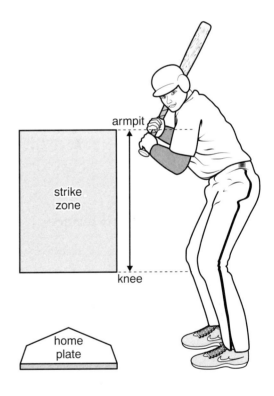

armpit

strike zone

knee

home plate

The strike zone for fast-pitch softball.

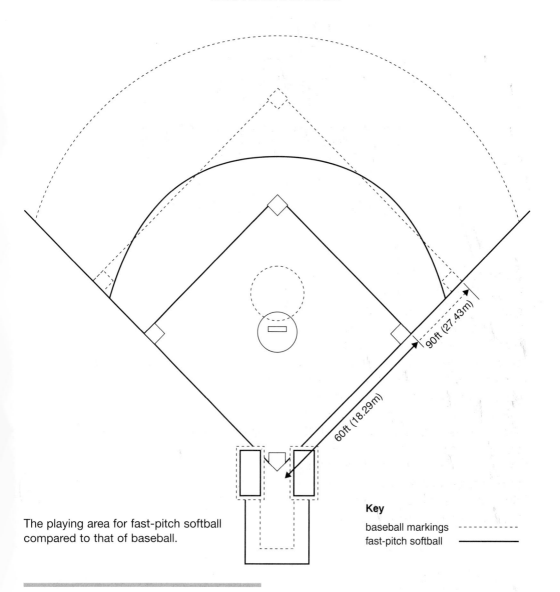

60ft (18.29m)

90ft (27.43m)

The playing area for fast-pitch softball compared to that of baseball.

Key

baseball markings ----------

fast-pitch softball ——————

🔴 PLAYING AREA

The shape of the field in fast-pitch softball is the same as in baseball. However, the size of the field is significantly smaller. The distance between the bases is 60ft (18.29m). For men, the distance from the pitching rubber to the home plate is 46ft (14.02m). For women, it is 40ft (12.19m). For softball, the ball is pitched from a flat surface, not off the mound as in baseball.

Yeh Hsiou-Ing of Taiwan – a fast-pitch pitcher in action.

● PITCHING

Before a pitch can be delivered, the ball must be presented to the batter. The pitcher must come to a complete stop, with the shoulders in line with first and third bases. The ball must be held in both hands, in front of the body. This position must be held for at least one second, but not more than ten seconds. The ball is held at waist level directly in front of the body. Both feet must be in contact with the pitcher's plate.

SLOW-PITCH SOFTBALL

Whereas baseball and fast-pitch softball are games dominated by pitching, slow-pitch softball is essentially a hitting game. Slow-pitch is played by single-sex and mixed teams. Unlike in fast-pitch and baseball, there are ten players in each slow-pitch team. The extra fielder plays in the outfield, and is called a rover.

The scoring system is exactly the same as in baseball and fast-pitch. A run is scored each time a player completes a circuit of the bases, touching each base in turn. The game is played over seven innings, with a coin toss deciding which team bats first.

● STRIKE ZONE

The strike zone in slow-pitch is larger than in fast-pitch, extending from the knees to the highest point of the

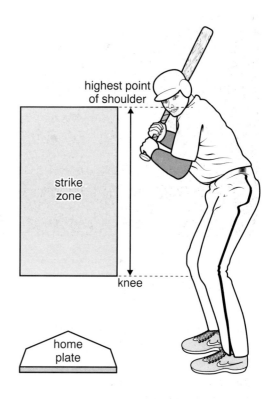

The strike zone for slow-pitch softball.

shoulder in the normal batting stance. Balls and strikes are called the same, but in slow-pitch the batter is out if the third strike is fouled off.

plate, or is hit by the batter. If the ball is not hit, all runners must return to base. If the runner fails to keep in contact with the base, he is called out.

● PLAYING AREA

The shape of the field is the same as for both baseball and fast-pitch. However, the infield area is slightly larger than the fast-pitch infield. The distance between the bases is 65ft (19.81m) and the distance from the pitching plate to the home plate is 46ft (14.02m). This is the case for male, female and mixed teams.

● STEALING

Unlike with baseball and fast-pitch, stealing is not allowed in slow-pitch. Base runners must stay in contact with the base until the ball reaches the

● PITCHING

Pitching in slow-pitch softball is a relatively easy skill. The fielding team must assume that every batter is going to hit the ball. It is the pitcher's job to force the batter to hit the ball in a certain way, i.e. either a ground ball or a fly ball, thereby giving the fielders the opportunity to make an appropriate play.

The pitched ball must travel in an arc with its highest point being between 6 and 12ft (1.83–3.66m) from the ground. This obviously prevents the pitcher delivering the ball too fast. Any pitcher delivering balls too fast is liable to be sent off the field.

The pitching trajectory in slow-pitch softball.

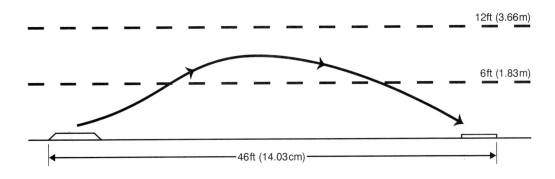

12ft (3.66m)

6ft (1.83m)

46ft (14.03cm)

Slow-pitch softball is a popular game. Pitching is quite easy, and the pitcher has to make the batter hit either a ground ball or a fly ball.

GLOSSARY

assist A throw to a team-mate enabling him to make a **put out**.

at bat Describes the player whose turn it is to bat.

balk An illegal action by the **pitcher** with a **runner** on **base**. As punishment, all the runners advance one base.

ball A **pitch** that does not enter the **strike zone**, and is not swung at by the **batter**.

base A base is sited at each corner of the **diamond**. There are four: first base, second base, third base and home.

base-on-balls If the **pitcher** throws four **pitches** outside the **strike zone**, and the **batter** does not swing, the batter is entitled to walk to first **base**. Base-on-balls are also called a walk.

base umpire The umpire who is responsible for calling one or more **bases.**

bases loaded First, second and third base are occupied when a batter is at bat.

batter The player **at bat**.

battery The combination of the pitcher and catcher.

batting average The **batter**'s average is calculated by the number of hits divided by the number of times **at bat**.

bench The area of the field where the teams sit. Also called the dugout.

bottom The second half of any **inning**.

breaking ball Any pitch that deviates in flight, e.g. a **curveball**, **slider**, or **knuckleball**.

bullpen Area of the field where **pitchers** warm up.

bunt When the **batter** allows the ball to hit the bat, creating a soft hit to the **infield**.

catch Where the fielder catches the ball in the air, without it touching the ground.

catcher The player who fields directly behind the **batter**.

catcher's box Area where the **catcher** must stay until the **pitcher** delivers the ball.

catcher's interference Where the **catcher** impedes the **batter**. The batter is awarded first base.

change up A slower **pitch**, usually thrown with the same motion as a **fastball**, thereby deceiving the **batter**.

choke up To hold the bat further up the handle.

count The number of **balls** and **strikes** the **batter** has received.

curveball A breaking **pitch** that curves in flight.

cut off A player who receives a throw from the **outfield**.

deadball When the ball is out of play.

designated hitter A **batter** who hits instead of the **pitcher**.

diamond The area created by the four bases.

double A two-base hit.

double header Where two games are played on the same day.

double play A play in which two players are **put out**.

error A fielding mistake that would have put a **runner** out.

fair ball A ball that is hit into **fair territory**.

fair territory The area of the field between the first and third baselines.

fastball A **pitch** thrown as fast as possible.

fly ball A ball that is hit into the air.

force play When a fielder retires a **runner** by touching the **base**.

forkball See **split fingered fastball**.

foul ball A ball that does not go into **fair territory**.

foul line One of the two lines marking the boundary between fair territory and foul territory.

foul territory The part of the field outside the first and third base lines, or **foul lines**.

foul tip A batted ball that goes sharply backwards and is caught by the **catcher**.

grand slam When a **batter** hits a **home run** with the **bases loaded**.

ground ball A ball that is hit along the ground.

ground rules Rules that make allowances for any field obstructions.

hit When a **batter** reaches **base** after hitting successfully.

home plate Where a batter stands when at bat.

home run When a **batter** hits the ball and completes a circuit touching all the **bases** without stopping.

infield The area of the field within the **diamond**.

infielder A player who fields in the **infield**.

inning When both teams have batted once, an inning is complete.

knuckleball A speciality **pitch** that deviates in flight.

line drive A hard-hit ball that travels directly on a line.

middle infielders Collective name for second baseman and the **shortstop**. Also called the pivot.

no hitter When no base hits are conceded by a **pitcher** throughout an entire game.

on-deck circle The area where the

next **batter** waits before it is his turn **at bat**.

out When the batting team have a player out. They have three outs per **inning**.

outfield The area of the field outside the **diamond** but still within the extension of the two **foul lines**.

outfielder A player who plays in the **outfield**.

passed ball When the **catcher** fails to field a **pitch** that should have been controlled, and **runners** advance on base.

pick off To catch a **runner** off base.

pinch hitter A substitute **batter**.

pinch runner A substitute **runner**.

pitch A ball delivered by the **pitcher** to the **batter**.

pitcher The player who delivers the ball to the batter.

pitch out A **pitch** deliberately thrown wide of the **plate**, to help the **catcher** throw out base stealers.

plate Abbreviation of **home plate**.

plate umpire The umpire who calls the balls and strikes from behind the home plate. Also known as the umpire-in-chief.

pop fly A ball that is hit high into the air and is caught by an **infielder**.

power alleys The space between the **outfielders**.

put out When a fielder retires an offensive player.

relief pitcher A substitute **pitcher**.

run A run is scored when a **runner** touches all **bases** in correct order.

run down When a **runner** is caught between **bases**.

runner An offensive player who is on or running towards any **base**.

shortstop One of the **infielders.**

screwball A speciality **pitch**.

single A successful hit that enables the **batter** to reach first base.

slider A **pitch** that breaks at the last minute.

split fingered fastball A **fastball** that dips at the last minute. Also called a forkball.

steal **Runners** can attempt to reach the next **base** whenever the ball is in play. This is called stealing.

strike A strike is a legal **pitch** if:
- the **batter** swings and misses;
- the ball passes through the **strike zone**;
- the ball is hit into **foul territory** (this only counts for the first two strikes);
- the ball hits the **batter** in the **strike zone**.

strike out When the **batter** has three **strikes**.

strike zone The area over **home plate** between the **batter**'s knees and chest.

switch hitter A **batter** who can hit both right- and left-handed.

tag When a fielder, while holding the ball, touches a base **runner**.

top The first half of an **inning**.

triple Where a **batter** reaches third **base** safely on one hit.

umpire-in-chief See **plate umpire**.

walk See **base-on-balls**.

wild pitch A **pitch** that is thrown so inaccurately that the **catchers** cannot field it.

USEFUL ADDRESSES

Amateur Softball Association of America
2801 NE 50th Street
Oklahoma City
Oklahoma 73111
Tel: 405-424-5266
Fax: 405-424-4734

Australian Baseball Federation
48 Atchison Street
St Leonards
NSW 2065
Australia
Tel: 2 437-4466
Fax: 2 437-4155

Baseball Canada
1600 James Naismith Drive
Suite 208
Ottawa
Ontario K1B 5N4
Tel: 613-748-5606
Fax: 613-748-5767

British Baseball Federation
PO Box 45
Hessle
East Yorkshire
HU13 0YT
United Kingdom
Tel: 01482 643551
Fax: 01482 640224
Website: http://www.bbf.org

British Softball Federation
PO Box 10064
London N6 5JN
United Kingdom

European Baseball Confederation
Thonetlaan 52
B-2050 Antwerp
Belgium
Tel/Fax: 3 219-0440

International Baseball Association
Avenue de Mon-Repos 24
Caisse Postale 131
1000 Lausanne 5
Switzerland
Tel: 21 311-1863
Fax: 21 311-1864

Irish Baseball & Softball Association
14 Innishmaan Road
Whitehall
Dublin 9
Ireland
Tel/Fax: 1 857-0450

Major League Baseball
350 Park Avenue
17th Floor
New York
NY 10022
United States of America
Tel: 212-339-7815
Fax: 212-758-8660

Major League Baseball International (Australia)
Level 4
120 Clarence Street
Sydney
NSW 2000
Australia
Tel: 2 299-7299
Fax: 2 299-4769

Major League Baseball International (Europe)
West Hill House
Suite 3
6 Swain's Lane
London
United Kingdom
Tel: 171 428-9988
Fax: 171 428-9990

New Zealand Baseball Federation
PO Box 97090
South Auckland Mail Centre 1730
New Zealand
Tel/Fax: 9 292-7436

South African Baseball Union
PO Box 751440
Gardenview
Johannesburg 2047
South Africa
Tel: 11 683-5722
Fax: 11 683-6457

USA Baseball
2160 Greenwood Avenue
Trenton
NJ 08609
United States of America
Tel: 609-587-2381
Fax: 609-587-1818
Website: http://www.usabaseball.com

INDEX